The Glacier's Wake

Katy Didden (signature)

Katy Didden

The Glacier's Wake

*For Pat and Puja —
with tremendous gratitude
for your friendship and
Thanks for inspiring poems!
Here's to many more
adventures.
Katy*

*2/23/14
Seattle* :)

Lena-Miles Wever Todd Poetry Series / Pleiades Press
Warrensburg, Missouri & Rock Hill, South Carolina

Published by Pleiades Press

Department of English
University of Central Missouri
Warrensburg, Missouri 64093

&

Department of English
Winthrop University
Rock Hill, South Carolina 29733

Distributed by Louisiana State University Press

Cover Image: *Albedo B14* (38" x 38"; polymer on linen) by Marek Ranis, 2004. Copyright © Marek Ranis. Used by permission of Marek Ranis.

Cover design by Kevin Tseng.
Interior design by Wayne Miller.
Author's photo by Jason Reblando.

2 4 6 8 9 7 5 3 1
First Pleiades Press Printing, 2013

Financial Assistance for this project has been provided by the Missouri Arts Council, a state agency.

**Missouri
Arts Council**
The State of the Arts

for my family

and in memory of my father
George A. Didden III

Contents

Acknowledgments

I would like to thank the editors of the following journals, anthologies, and websites where these poems (some in different versions) first appeared:

6x5—Tense Forms Journal: "Ode to the Ear"

Bat City Review: "The Sycamore on Balance"

Best New Poets 2009: "String Theory: Pyramus and Thisbe"

B O D Y: "The Sycamore on Forgiveness" and "The Glacier on Middle-Age"

Crab Orchard Review: "Before Edison Invented Lights," and "Lopez Island"

Crazyhorse: "Pleasure Milker"

Delmarva Review: "Skyline" and "Market Day Outside the Walls of Tangiers"

Ecotone: "The Sycamore on Praise"

Hayden's Ferry Review: "Los Globos" (now "The Fire Balloons")

Image: "The Wasp on Weddings," "The Wasp on Kierkegaard," "The Wasp on Renaissance Painters," "The Wasp on Archangels"

Jabberwock Review: "Peace Tower," and "Glacier" (now "The Glacier's Wake")

The Journal: "Nest"

The Kenyon Review: "The Soldier on Routine," and "The Model Composure of the Dead"

Pleiades: "Excavating the Cyclops' Eyesocket"

Poetry: "At Chartres," and "Embrace Them All"

Shenandoah: "Mind's-Eyed Island"

Smartish Pace: "Arriving at Ubehebe Crater, We Sing The Sound of Music," and "Lamoille County Field Days"

Witness: "The Penitentes' Morada"

Thanks to the editors at *Verse Daily*, for featuring "Nest" and selecting it as a "2009 Favorite." Thanks also to the editors at *Poetry Daily* for reprinting "The Soldier on Routine" and "The Sycamore on Balance."

Several of these poems appear on dorothyprizes.org. I would like to say a special thanks to Mary Rosenberg and the Dorothy Prize coordinators for their generous support and encouragement over the years.

For their kindness, insight, and inspiring talent, I would like to thank my teachers: Jennifer Atkinson, Carl Phillips, Elizabeth Arnold, Michael Collier, Stanley Plumly, Lynne McMahon, Scott Cairns, and Aliki Barnstone.

I have met wonderful friends as a result of studying poetry. The final drafts of these poems evolved out of many hours of dialogue and conversation, and I am grateful to my friends for their thoughtful attention to these poems. I would like to thank all the writers at the University of Maryland, especially Charlie Clark, Shara Lessley, Brian Moylan, and Ali Stine. Thanks to my Chicago friends, Vicky Anderson and Rachel Webster, for feedback and stellar company. Thanks to everyone at The University of Missouri, especially the poets who gave moral support as I wrote most of these poems: Stefanie Wortman, Jessica Garratt, Marc McKee, Claire McQuerry, Chad Parmenter, Melissa Range, Austin Segrest, Stephanie Wortman, and (honorary poet) Arijit Sen. I would like to say a special thank you to Joanne Diaz, whose generosity, sense of humor, and dedication to hard work inspire me, and whose editorial suggestions improved these poems a hundred fold.

I would also like to thank several individuals who read drafts of this manuscript and offered brilliant advice: Charlie Clark, John Nieves, Gabriel Fried, and Megan Snyder-Camp.

I am indebted to the Bread Loaf Writers Conference, The Vermont Studio Center, The Virginia Center for Creative Arts, and The Hambidge Center for providing inspiration and support as I wrote this book.

I am very grateful to The University of Maryland and The University of Missouri for academic fellowships that greatly facilitated the writing of this book. I would also like to thank St. Louis University for a Postdoctoral Fellowship in the Micah Program, which gave me both time and a positive environment for completing these poems. Special thanks to all of my wonderful students as well.

I would like to thank my friends in D.C., St. Louis, Seattle, Columbia, and Chicago for providing some of the material for these poems, and for being such fine individuals.

I'd like to thank Marek Ranis for letting us feature his stunning painting for the book cover. Thanks also to my dear friend, photographer Jason Reblando, for lending his time and talent with the author photo. Special thanks for Kevin Tseng, who designed the book cover, and whose friendship, wit, and insight are a true joy.

Thanks to Melissa Kwasny for selecting this manuscript as the winner of the Lena Miles Wever Todd Prize. Thanks also to Susan Ludvigson, Wayne Miller, Kathryn Nuernberger, and everyone at Pleiades Press for believing in these poems and for giving the book such careful attention. It has been an honor to work with such an outstanding editing team while preparing this book.

Finally, I'd like to thank my family for their constant love and encouragement. These poems are for you.

The Glacier's Wake

Tooth-snout, blue eye, white-tongued as icy Jove
on a god-slow lay,

as alive as how I thought my grief should be—
a heaving ice field, an evaporating history

onto which, inside the crags of which,
I liked my mind to climb.

Down where the cold erases the weather's structure,
where ice eclipses

the too-wide sky, I waited in a cell of air
for the year to melt each brittle inch

into what's green—the growing sea,
the wind-scummed water mirror

with clouds I read as words from my loved dead.
By my own heat, I melted room to hold my body.

I made a god of birds out of the man.

~1~

Pleasure Milker

—Iguazu Falls, Argentina

You're the kind who stands still
in front of awful things and squints
as though you could see into
the god chambers of every atom in every
drop of water. O! Maw of Fog.
O! Foam Throat. It's hard to stare
at such a changing thing. Peel the surface
and the falls funnel back to drops,
jungles flee to seed—all that's left
is lithosphere, scarred as it is.
Nothing to blaze the fix. Which
brings you to the time of lava.
Just a girl, the earth's a short-winged
planet, hurtled shuddering
along her ellipse, humming slow
twenty octaves below middle E.
She flies low over the poor yards
of stars, fanning her boiling
organisms and polishing the dried char
off molten rock with still-glistening wings.
Soon, the ice-tipped spine. Soon, fire-
singe of feathers, a fringe of green
below the chin. By now, drenched
as a fern, you resurface to the thundering
gush of falls. You filmy pilgrim,
you pleasure milker, you open your mouth
to sing as though it were a living thing.
The old girl's gone to peat. You're slick
with rain and heat and lift your feet
into the fragile air. But there's a record here,
under the white veils of the river.

Mind's-Eyed Island

Earth's newest island is Surtsey.
   It erupted above sea level in 1963,
signaling in smoke, settling over the sea

in a slope of scoria—an island, we've decided,
   where we're not allowed to live: only seals and fulmars,
guillemots and whooper swans.

In uninhabited ocean, Surtsey's eruption
   harmed no one, and no one harms islands
on purpose, but then a booted foot,

a field of untrod ash. It is hard to leave be
   what the law ropes off. Before signatures
on mainland pages paired the rim of Surtsey

with a hefty fee, a rebounding belt of ethics,
   reporters for *Paris Match* left southwest Iceland
for the newest shore along the Mid-Atlantic fissure.

They stayed fifteen minutes before the roaring,
   airborne ash and fire scared them back.
Then the eruption echoed in ink—

a surface to people with willow, rock pillow,
   algae, sea— they staked claims for the sake
of merely having seen. Little Surtsey adds itself to the world,

brimming with news from the core. Her name is fire,
   she's an ingot, she's a blot. She's the coda of the long song
ice and fire sing. I watched Surtsey be born again online—

the wing of a plane in the frame against Surtsey's
　　plume of steam, its billowing flag of cumulus
upping the clear skies, hazing its gray over the sun.

All that's taken root arrived in the bellies of birds
　　and seals: this is the fifteenth anniversary
of the discovery of a single earthworm burrowing itself

through Surtsey's increasingly nutritious soil.
　　The island erupts in thought—
a little boat over the blank reaches its resistance—

and I'm glad there's somewhere we can't wreck,
　　where earth's beginning gets re-set. At the place
we can never see, where we'll never set our feet,

grow ideas. Imagine how we'd hew a place to sleep
　　out of the solid rock that waves won't rock.
Moss under the shadow of the albatross,

and ash-halved boulders of pumice—
　　Oh how they look like a cluster of huts
that would shelter the body from sun and dust.

String Theory: Pyramus and Thisbe

Scientists say the key is gravity—its arc of motion
extends beyond perception into a million cosmos

mirroring our own. If it would woo concurrency
through our dimension's scrim, I'd shape the way

things weigh into a word, and send new worlds
a sign made from the undrawn lines of apples.

Just thinking of simultaneity, amplified to the nth degree,
totally floors me. It is like knowing the pyramids exist,

though I have never seen them, their shadow sides wearing smooth
under the sole of the millionth stealthy foot,

while climbers scaling glaciers free another cold jade inch
for fish, and high on Mauna Loa tourists print the tread of rubber tires

onto fresh-cooled ash as they wheel oceanwards down Earth's
volcanic spine, and how all this is happening while I'm asleep in DC,

and somewhere else, out of reach, you're turning in the night
towards your wife. If I could tap the wall of all for points permeable,

I'd set my ear against a seam and cull clues of alt-you,
alt-I. What's the shape of the world where we are happy?

A place where it's still not strange for me to rest
against the length of you, say on the dunes of a slow-

paced oasis in the mirror of whose water moves the sky,
where cloud or bird's the winking of an eye, and where

the wave-work of mirage blurs the shape of children
racing figure-eights around the palms. In the beauty of their bodies

you can see the trace resemblance of Thisbe, who, in the plot's alt-tale,
never feared the blood-jawed lion, already fed,

but waited clear-eyed, clean-veiled, until the lion left,
and in real fields beyond the wall met Pyramus

at the tomb of Ninus, under the moonlit branches
of the white mulberry, where he sat brewing tea,

munching an apple—food of certainty, symbol for
the harmony of all dimensions layered skin to skin,

of how all things begin, and how, fearless of falling,
one who left Paradise

wriggles in again.

The Glacier on the Close-Up

Say you see interiors
(bright blue,
where the water moves)—

still, zoom is hell
on the weathered.

When I was smooth as glass
I was a starlet—
the mirror of Mars—

now merely a shield
beaming light
on the body of Venus.

The Sycamore on Praise

A way to stay put is to feel Earth
tilting—to know its vast surface curves,
that the sky's brightening is not the sun
flattering you with its attention,
just the speed at which you're spinning west.
You're a speck. You aren't meant to last.
Seeing death everywhere, you can choose
despair, blunt your roots on rocks, accuse
the cold wind as it lashes your limbs
then train your shape to the synonym
for "whip." You can rip the sky to skim
water. Or, you can watch yourself change,
marvel how death mottles you with strange
spots, wrinkles your skin and plumps your veins.
In the shade, you can love what repeats—
branched river and snake tracks in the leaf,
the fruit dangling like suspended suns,
the years' cycling, the slant-rhymed seasons—
or the heron, like a gray beacon
on the same high limb each afternoon—
our daily habits, hearing a tune
in thunder, words in the shaking leaves.
Praise the stuttering flow of light off waves.
Praise the linking wind, the sudden rain's
promise that what was will be again.
Praise lush soil, praise infinite patterns
of which you're made, to which you will return.

Before Edison Invented Lights

if you stood outside at night
at a moonless hour
you could mark your place in the universe
by how you fit
among the field of stars.
The world was colder then,
and the distances between
one family and another
were bigger by an exponent,
which meant people traveled more,
if they didn't go as far.
Anyone who watches a bird flying—
a small bird especially—
and sees it rise in full flight
like a voice shifting octaves, knows
that you can get anywhere
if you only imagine the connecting line
between where you are
and where you'd like to go.
A stone on a stone makes a wall,
an arch in a tower holds a bell,
the air in the bell catches sound
and the wind carries it
over the lake
where it fills the white sail.
You navigate by stars.
Between the stars
are more stars you can't see,
and between all stars is a dark silence
and the great pull
we only understand as longing,
to which we're tuned like bells,
over which our eyes draw lines

between the bright places.
We give the blackness shapes
with names of gods.
In a fist-sized glass dome,
in a vacuum atmosphere not unlike the universe,
Edison, after many trials, suspended
a filament of straight bamboo
whittled down to its threads
then charred by heat
until it resembled the stuff of stars.
It burned for six hundred hours,
and the ceilings of our dreams
lost their dim flickerings,
to the steady glow of incandescence.
And now, whole cities shine up
like planets, and most stars,
to our eyes, have gone out.
Unless you travel.
In the North Cascades, on a ridge
overlooking a white volcano,
the only thing darker than the night
is the gliding shadow of a great owl.
When you sleep with your face to the sky
the stars are not so much above
as around you. Stare long enough
and you begin to feel
you could lift your body off the earth
and hover in the black night
on the web of your awe
at a billion suns
towards which
everything you're made of yearns.

Ode to the Ear

I rolled in like a skater
gliding rims I was

the sound of the sea I
was wind I plunged

with the echo of oceans
into a marsh of wax

under a dark ceiling
at the center I sang

little wind little sea
unsink me unsound me

I'm beating a drum where
one word could drown me

On Love: A Debate with Three Finns

They taught me to speak with the middle third
of my lips, as if I'd sucked a lemon, or as if my mouth
were frozen slightly open. After "Good morning,"
"Nice to meet you," and "Where is the sauna?"

I asked them how to say "I love you." At this,
they murmured to each other. Then Satu,
the most outspoken of the three
who often said things that were slightly shocking,

said she didn't know how to translate *love* exactly.
In English, she said, you use the word too lightly.
You say "I love you" to your mother, your friend,
and your lover, to a lover you only slightly more than like,

to a lover you hope will never leave you.
How do you ever know, she wondered, which love
your lover means? At first, I thought it was
a question of degree. I measured "I love you"s

by the way my lover looked at me. The context
mattered; *love* was true, since love shifts intensity,
since any lover is both friend and mother sometimes.
But then she said the word for love

Finns rarely say; they speak it to one person only,
or at most to very few. My friends grew serious,
as if the vastness of the word had swallowed speech.
I asked if any of them had ever said it.

By their looks, I understood none of them knew
what the others would say, and that no Finn
would ever ask this question. But they answered me
shyly, each explaining whom she'd said it to,

and I knew somehow the word involved the body,
that the body was what made it irrevocable.
What grief could I have spared if I had faced that choice
with the man I loved then? I would have said the word.

Knowing the word, I also would have known
how to love totally. And he, on the verge of a life with me,
would have whispered only some variant of *like*,
and the clarity of *like* would have set us free.

The Penitentes' Morada

—Abiquiu Pueblo, NM

Building with three waist-high windows
their shutters locked from the outside—
small latches, those Ulysses bonds
that hold the monks back, though the desert
surges forward with its heat
and infiltrates the shutter-cracks with light—
as if those muted beams were all
they could withstand—
the way the body, always seeking
oblivion, feels light's tug,
would step out of the adobe walls
and, reeling from the spectrum,
sink into sand. Were the monks inside,
their minds were wholly sky;
no cage exists without its opposite.
The mind is always elsewhere, won't stay put.
Whose merciful hands, then,
could bind us to our longing?

Peace Tower

In the year my father died
Yoko Ono built a beam of light

on a grass-covered island
across a narrow field of ocean

from Reykjavik. You should see it—
click this link: see the shape

that started as thoughts of a line
in Yoko's mind. When Yoko told

John her idea for the light,
he wanted it to shine up from his yard.

So now in air no one can own, the way
no one really owns a tune, a light burns

that bullets cannot stop. I'd like to fly
to Iceland, take a boat to the beam.

I'd like to see every flake of snow
set aglow as it fell. Against the aggregate

of light, I'd take the hailing bright
as mute replies from my beloved dead.

Imagine trying to sing to someone
through a wall of mud, a mile

of sea. John's voice sings across
the century—can still be heard

in earth's remotest cities. The plunk
of the piano that his fingers traveled over

imprinted onto grooves of vinyl
over which the needles spiral, so sound

spins up into the air. Let the beam
spiral off a low cyclonic system

funneling the sky over Iceland,
two opposing forces like the thread-

down of sound into sense, like the balance
of scales of a Libra singing, his voice

in key, bending melody. The beam of light
is white in the mind, blue in fact.

The base of the light is white glass.
Heat from the core melts the black

sand of Iceland to something smooth,
translucent: earth that lets light

shine through. In my mind,
I see the beam warbling up to the sky.

At times the beam is wide, at times
it thins, at times it seems to stutter

over light-erasing mist, as if light
were a held luck we shine up to the dark,

in the winter, under whistling stars.

The Glacier on Middle-Age

The threat of death breathes its heat
on your neck, softens your features,
finally teaches
your youth to you.

The inner light that shone in your face
is snuffed by a rough powder,
by boot scuffs.

Yet compression gives
an age-obscuring gleam—
a startling blue.
Your beauty is now up to you.

On Hearing of the Trend for Sexy Chamber Music Trios

Lean your body
into mine
  as I lean back

against the hills
of Nelahozeves.
  You the hollow body,

me the bow
across your back.
  Inside you, me,

inside me
sound, as a bell
  at the pull

of a hand
or the fill
  of the wind.

Arc in when I
arc back,
  bind my arms

with arms
and hum
  your song

inside my ear.
Let river in,
  let leaves

on air be over us,
snug to the hollows
   of you, let me.

No longer one,
we're three
   as three encircle

all ways one—
inside, around,
   between, among—

let melody untwine,
go split,
   let what was me

be three
but mute:
   one under waves, one

held in chains, and one
who plies the glim
   supine, the glinting

spine of you,
split too,
   in tune, inrooted

wingless on the green
under and above
   the leaves, bent back

on the hill
under waves
   in the sway

of the wind's
wild measure
 and the rain-

joined rays of sun.
 Come back, love,
here, love,
in-hum, come.

The Wasp on Weddings

—Wasp, genus "Hymenopterae"
— "Hymenaeus," the God of Weddings

These days we gods
are diminished things,
  black winged.

I float
like the infinitesimal
  hesitation,

the unheard breath
after I:
  "I *wasp* will."

"I *wasp* do."
I hover over
  the first course

of figs.
In the old days,
  the homage

of corsets,
now the callas'
  attenuating stems,

the bridesmaids
in blue with white
  sashes, the bride

divided by the arm
of the groom
  at her waist—

as if she would break
in two.

"Embrace Them All"

—Parc Georges Brassens, Paris

Most afternoons, I'd run laps through Parc Brassens
where grows the second smallest vineyard

I have ever seen, and where those silver,
pruned-back stalks looked blunt,

strung-out on wires, and mostly dead
all winter. That was how I saw them.

That's all I expected. Even in the cold,
I'd see a guy my age there, once a week,

playing his guitar. He'd sit next to the bench
where I'd be stretching. He rarely spoke—

just to ask if I'd like a song—
until the week before I left for good.

I was sitting at the top of a hill
about a hundred feet away from where

if you stand tiptoe you can see the Eiffel Tower.
He sat too close to me. We spoke of many things.

Then he suggested we go at it right there,
on the ground, under the sun. This is how

one lives who knows that she will die:
rolling in the arms of anyone she can—

rolling in the arms of a musician—aware
that no one cares much what we do

in little knolls behind reedy forsythia,
in the middle of a Tuesday, in the middle

of living. And I would know now
how he felt, and the ground against me,

and whether he was rough or sweet.
And what is possible would widen every hour.

Oh, but me, I thought I was immortal.

Northwest Passage

Variations of glacial greens and blues—
for hundreds of years, an iceberg's poised to move,
and when it breaks loose, it flows slowly,
adding its enormity to the sea,
the swell only perceptible as an inching up of emerald
on the gangplank of a wreck.

*

Old Worthies in the narrows, striking for the utter North,
believing that the lid of the world was liquid,
set course through shifting archipelagos for the wild
north's source. But the ship ran aground
on the "Polar Sea"—the sea more a skull,

and the bergs (opaled, auroreal) its vacant glance,
almost hospitable, the shadow-eyed obelisks
transmuting with a crack.

When the mast snapped, these men
extended the edge of the world,
recording their fate on a single sheet of paper
they would bury, then dig up again
as the months wore on—
the fine black script covering the margins.

*

Dear men on *The Terror*, we've received your letter.
It seems you're aware that your mission was in error.
As for a Strait through the North, few care—
we steer by satellite. It's the ice we're after.

Like you, we confuse awe at grandeur for hunger,
and feel less terror at the world
than at what's in us: thirst
and fear of smallness
(both ours and Earth's).

While we're stalled in quagmires of what to wear
(boiled wool or gauze, fur or thinnest linen),
earth contracts on its axis, cueing epics:

and the hero who creeps up the Alp, ice-picks a divot,
sends the peak shale a-rolling back home to the ocean, sweats.
The waters are rising; we'd like to exchange
your out-and-back adventure for an ark.

In an effort to reach you, I've sent this by mail
through a green-skied squall, using precious fuel.
In place of address, I've listed coordinates:
a frozen maze, heat-crazed, and a giant iceberg,
beneath which it's rumored the last of you huddled for heat.

We've christened it "the monument"—
to bravery, to your lost bodies, to the fierceness of your will,
or else to folly, as heat returns
all written words to water.
The passage clears. The far shore blurs.

The Wasp on Archangels

It is possible
to enter a room
 silently,

appear in the air,
instill fear,
 literally slip

through the inch
under screens
 or ram your wings

at the glass
as if you could pass
 straight to light.

~2~

Avalanche

Survivors say the snow
goes wild as whitewater
and you swim.

When the snow halts
you don't know
which way is up

and you cannot move
anyway, not your
thumb or your chin,

not to blink, not even
to fill your lungs.
Begin "a," begin "v"

valanca, valanga
the word source: lava—
Italian for torrent,

for gully, for what
engulfs us. Years ago
two lovers died

near Innsbruck—bride
and groom, on honeymoon
from Argentina.

Her name was Liliana.
We visit her tomb—
exquisite as a mosque

with point-arched windows—
most delicate of all in Recoleta.
The guide says Liliana

lived a while in India,
that her father chose
her shroud: a red sari

covering her, in the coffin
in the crypt. I think how
she must have loved

the feel of the Himalayas
underfoot. She named
her dog Sabu :

"a charming village
with a small gompa….
North of Leh

in the Nubra Valley….
once thought to be
under a huge glacier."

To be under a glacier.
To be not under, but
inside ice. *Nubra*

translation: *Ldhumra*
translation: the valley of flowers.
Where ice melts back

yellow lilies bloom,
hem-stitching the black soil
with seeds, and "the grass

is starred with white anemones,"
gentling the declivity.
The guide says Sabu

died too—on the very day,
eight thousand miles away
in Buenos Aires—as though

the dog set off
across the mileless white light
of a threshold.

Now the form they were
(but bronze) shadows
blooms, presses against

the air; oil-dark, their sheen
pulls heat from snowless skies
above Buenos Aires.

My father, beside me, names
the plants: "That tree
is not a tree. See how thorn-canes

wrap the statue's base?"
"Yes." "A Rose."
(Rose, rune, cane, thorn).

"See the purple bud?" "Yes."
"Dianthus." (Carnation,
coronation, crown). *Bloom*

and thorn over bronze feet.
The scorned stalks sway.
"These are the leaves

of a Canna lily" Canna (Gr)
means Kanes [cane],
a mat of reeds, called Pride of India,

or in Thailand a symbol
for Father's Day.
Oh shiny-eyed old man

leaning forward
like you've seen
stone angels move,

is it you or I will go first?
How will the earth
not shatter by that parting?

Snowfields slid and weight-
loosed boulders wrecked the air
with sound, destroying

what had been a sturdy roof,
a shield. Then darkness came
and stilled the pines,

the trills of birds—
Hear thunder cease.
See snow, like silence,

suffocate the scene.
In seconds, under
the perilous slope, by snow

the valley of light
went black. *Are you dead
or sleeping? who could*

prick, from ice, your pulse?
I won't withstand
slow blood's false death,

exhume skin scarred
by its own hand.
I will not bury you alive.

From the French: *À Val*
"Towards the valley."
The snow rushed in

like water. *Avaler:*
"To swallow." The snow
rushed in like air. A throat,

the torrent filled the throat.
Her hand was on the door,
but her hand had turned

to marble. *No air, asleep*
(the ice!)—beside you black,
inside you snow,

there where the level
of the valley grows, I'll vigil.
Under everything is

ocean; under oceans, ore,
a sphering, obscuring
death. In the seed, in soil,

in the seabed (thrust
to peaks), in the lush-grass
green roll of valleys,

there was always
the danger of your dying.
Who'll cross first?

Did her image rise before him
like stale light? How long
did he, in disbelief,

outlive her? Grief in the A-line
of her dress, in the body's
narrow bell. Grief

in the resting hand (so thin!)
and the leaves of lilies,
bending. Grief in the thrust

of her chin, shaping the front
of a word. Grief in the curve
of the rail, down to her crypt,

and on each bright step a tile
like a lit path out.
My father traces his hand

on the inscription: *Perché*
(why?) *Perché* (why?).
Her body froze

in a sudden wall of ice.
If not by snow, in sleep,
in wilderness nearer to

the sky and blinding storms,
the wall of ice is only
death. My father's secret

blood, cancered, starves
the body blood should feed.
Leuco (white); *cell* (room

where monks dwell).
The white cells fill
the blood (*interstice*

of ice). *Poesis* (to make);
hyper (over, above, beyond;
to step over, cross). *Who'll*

cross first? Lymph (Gr. pseudo
nymph (ancient) for bride;
semi-divine, spirit).

Inside the blood (like snow)
the cancer grows—
hollowing the bones.

Song for whom the gods
take back. If it's me the statue
shadows, it blocks the light

and lets me lift my eyes.
I've watched my father die.
Behold, the valley

once was ice and where we stand
was glacier. A past—the weight
of years—vanishes here.

When clouds break, see
what the sun turns blue?
and for whom?

Some cup a hand
over the mouth,
exchanging the oxygen

of their own breath
in the little hand cave
until it runs out.

Survival depends
on the proximity
of witnesses.

Sometimes a blue
the mind can hardly grasp
is of our earth delights us.

There was always the danger
of your dying. Chill the walls,
in the quiet (swept),

where we come
to adore the dead.
Cornice bricks

sift to sand, the angels'
hands, the steep-roofed tombs
under wings of pale brown doves.

I will not bury you alive.

Outside the walls,
crowding the streets,
old men are blooming.

Under the shade trees,
they dream. How green!
and how gentle! the grasses.

The Fire Balloons

—New Year's Eve, Buenos Aires

The world falls in the yard
fireless—a dim,
harmless thing.
Terry rushes over

with long hands,
reads the creases
on the world
and folds it in on itself.

Under bomb and blaze
he carries it
tucked beneath his arm:
a shard, a wing.

At Chartres

Who wielded the chisel
at the left portal,
south porch, the scene

of Theo chained,
naked to the waist, leaning in
to the brutal hand

of what looks to be
an even younger boy?
What man carved stone

to mimic flesh
as it would look inside
the torture of its flensing?

How he must have held
the scene in his own
mind, thought it back

to the act itself,
modeling the lines
with his own limbs

so he would know
both how a body
bends in pain, and how

a hand extends the flayer's rake.

The Wasp on Renaissance Painters

Imagine the Virgin
imagining figs.

Paint a Mary
who stares
  at a plate

of sliced figs.
Imagine the cherubs
  imagining figs.

Imagine green, Capuchine
yellow, imagine
  mercurial vermilion

in the black background
of a body,
  see my oiled wing

as the armor of Romans
who grip,
  in the post-kiss

of Judas,
the luminous
  curser of figs.

The Soldier on Routine

We are living with the young Christ
   in the green zone. Even we who are not He
suffer hands tugging our hems,

though our minds select the bodies
   we see. Young Christ is dual,
but what of Him is like us is, like us,

taken in by order: the roof and walls,
   the roof and walls, inside which we sleep—
boot scuffs and dust, the white floors wiped clean.

He does not eat, some days, and so too
   we choose, and can. It's not that this
isn't hell, though the lamp-switch lights

long into the night. If we could name
   the mindframe *sight*, the body *wall*,
a solid feature with a latch, through which

we exit, armored, to disorder, that is, Ur—
   the original being, or its pre-becoming.
Out there the zone is we, the tank

a brutal country, singing. Young Christ
   is dual, though even the god He is
won't interfere. The cells beneath the surface

of the seen he says he senses like his own
   skin, still unflayed. That scrim in him,
keeping him human, among us crimping

barbed wires over buildings. Our hands
    bleed, but then we've made a thing
and can put it from us. If only they'd stay far

from us, or else we infiltrate a mind—
    walking in on the backs of the uttered
word, a word shook loose through

the terrifying bodies, where every pore's
    unbarriered. A hand nailed to a house,
the pierced room a cage, the wound a seam

we fill with seed. Body in which we live
    unsafe, and then He breaks through to
two at once, and this by violence. We who

are not He cannot contain it. Schism of many-
    chambered brain, schism of time, schism
of no into infinite pain, amnesia of the known,

of where we were before and if we're where
    was Eden, where's the latch? Where are
leaves to cover all these bodies? We watch

our hands in motion widening the wound—
    it's there we enter, as though we could pass through
to the princeless, incinerated kingdom.

The Sycamore on Balance

A symmetry of forces, yes
but not of shape. The roots: a mess
of curves. Like slow snakes
they incorporate
rocks. With full weight press-

ing down, my trunk arrows skywards.
For humans, centering's awkward.
You lack longevity,
can't fight gravity,
grow heavy. What wayward

cantilevering keeps you calm?
When sorrow settles, blights your limbs,
what dark contortions
fix you to the source?
Contrition. The light-aimed psalm.

Planetarium

—*The Natural History Museum, NYC*

Spun steel apes the stars—
museum astray in metal.
Clare runs up the ramp,
laps the sun on the slant
rim of Saturn. She spirals
near the rail, animates the plan
that what seems, is—map of time,
God's atelier, he who strum-
tunes the spheres in the ether-
stream, unsettles the pall
when winter tints the sunlit panes
to pale. In our ears, the aria
of Mars, a trumpet, a minaret,
tears the seams of minutes,
stills the spheres. Clare tires.
Tears mar her star-rapt aura, spill.
Her steps sputter in the near-inert
measure of terrapins. Earth turns,
time inters us, simple materials all,
still reaping time-lent elements
for rare allures (palettes of pearl,
the sea's innate salts) as the sun
in raiments of mist serrates seen
with unseen. Let the mute umpire,
who nips our stint, relent—
snap the starlit tarp, unstun the air
in sleet. In lapis pleats, as she sleeps,
let Clare—who illuminates
rooms—assume the eternal.
Unnail the plane for the aerial.
Let elation be netless, elliptical.

Lamoille County Field Days

—Johnson, Vermont

From the bright square of light just inside the barn door,
the Craft Show cashier looks out at the crowd
through thick-lensed glasses on which the mist
has dried not quite invisibly, so everything she sees
blurs gently, and the youngsters glow in small haloes
of heat. They gather round, waist-high to a volunteer,
who fills ten baby bottles with whole milk,
and fastens a rubber nipple to each cap. Above them all,
out across the field, the fog stalls at the foothills—
the gray arm of a farmer scattering tiny seeds of water,
which saturate the air and, under the pavilion,
curl the thinning hair of the hypnotist who breathes
"Relaaax" into a mic and snaps, so that a rugged man
on stage, counting to ten, omits the six, and curtsies
at the crowd before he sits. And while the girls race,
swigging the milk through pinholes in the nipples,
the giant Belgian horses chew the red fence that corrals them,
and the cashier slips out the back of the barn and wanders
behind the white tents to the farthest fencepost
where the field dips down toward the Gihon and she can see
the fog reaching up to the ghost-height of the ice, eons ago,
that shaped this place and packed the soil into a fertile valley.
And the fog!—it looks so lovely, erasing the ridge and making
even the nearest mountain strange, as the wind opens
a fringe of dark patches, and the black paved road
winds up the slope to disappear in mist. She stares
like she'll be quizzed for details later, when she turns back
towards the fairgrounds, the whole town gathered there,
moving like a sugar-seeking river, like a sweaty sea
that barely registers when it shifts to make room for her.

Market Day Outside the Walls of Tangiers

(on an oil painting by Louis Comfort Tiffany)

Without the glossiness of glass,
what good is color?
Who loves a hat

that looks the same
as all the others?
Figures on glass

get the gravitas of weather,
all the allusion
of the shifting sun—

but these men won't
inflate on light,
won't take a look of insight

when rays travel
like a wave
of traded news.

Perpetual noon's
a kind of gloom.
The glazier refuses

to finesse this—
keeps paint spare—
the wall is threadbare,

so is the air,
and his palette
is a paint-by-numbers:

wares in the burlap sack
on the back of the ox
are strips off the roof

of the minaret,
or bits a blade curled
off the door to the market.

The mule's foreleg,
the window lintel,
the swaddled brim of turbans,

clouds and stones:
all touched with sun-defying white
in dots the eye alights on

like a bee. The mind unlocks
in this economy,
where men wear robes of sky and sea.

The Glacier on Lack of Sleep

When day comes, the light's
too bright.

A yawn forms behind the spires
of your eyes. Your jaw
cracks, splits a crevasse.
Little parts of you collapse.

If you were older
or cared less about being seen

you would lie down in public.

The Model Composure of the Dead

—Recoleta Cemetery, Buenos Aires

Pale-brown doves stutter-whoop in the pines—
the morning light casts long shadows on the stones
of this miniature city. Groundsmen in gray coveralls
scrub select mausoleums, then sit on concrete benches
trading smokes. As a joke, one tips grave water
on the other's shoes—he shrinks from it as from infection—
water spills in thick black streams across the paths
of dull-eyed feral cats and pools under the marble feet
of angels. On the only tour in English, the guide
apologizes for the crumbling tombs. The families
of the dead neglect their dues. Dust gathers
on the little altars, strewn with dried blooms,
and enormous cobwebs hang in corners no breeze stirs.

*

Outside the cemetery, there's a two-hundred-year-old
rubber tree, its trunk wide as a house. Limbs stretch
over half a city block, propped by two-pronged stilts,
and broad, shiny leaves curl over the patios of three cafes.
Its roots tangle the sewer pipes and hold the earth together
under the stalls of silver matte cups and carved
and polished jungle birds, under the white
Franciscan church and the Museum of Fine Arts,
under the Hotel Guido and its two passenger elevator,
under the perfume billboards along Avenida 9 de Julio.
The roots reach all the way to the Atlantic,
and the roots grow around the Recoletan crypts
like a nest, and if such things are possible, they carry
the local gossip, amplified from the canopy of vinyl,
down to the slumbering ears of the old powers
who reply with fat figs that thwack the café tables
like little bombs, threatening the tea cups.

~3~

Lopez Island

When I should have left off grieving,
I carried you with me across the water.

I listened to the rock crabs
burrow in the sand. They scritched their claws

along the underbellies of rocks—
the sound of lines.

The tides' sound rolled, was round, refrained.

The crabs were green—
like the sea—

with oily shadows at the joints
like the backs of waves.

I'd lift the rocks
and watch them flee the sun.

Nest

*(found on a branch between the handrails
of the tourist bridge, Iguazu Falls, Argentina)*

Yellow bill, deft needle
braid of reeds and thistle.
Oval in the white sway:

a branch (a dumb place),
a shell the human finger
soils. Mishandled little

wilderness, the nest.
Holy, the ground. How
to loosen the straps

(unlearned) how open
our ears for warning? We
set the branch aswing.

The bird (foolish thing)
flickers through the bush.
Yahweh wing, scissoring,

no tablet, no commandment,
no chalked circumference
around the wild, signaling

"stand back." The mega lens
descends (hand numb to flame).
And click. And crack.

Arriving at Ubehebe Crater, We Sing
The Sound of Music

—Death Valley, California

"Baby, you're on the brink." Rolf, to Liesl

We like to mock the way Christopher Plummer
sings the last syllable of "Edelweiss,"
how he doesn't sing "weiss" so much as
breathe into it with a puff of vacancy.
You can find the whole meaning
of the film in that bit, the loss
of a known country, the captain o'erthrown,
surprised into love by the songs of a nun.
Our jaws lock operatically in the "O"
of shock or orgasm, the same shape
of the earth when it registers eruption,
as here—a big bowl of a crater,
its gorgeous alluvial fans draping
the red-tinted rills. In the seconds
it takes us to sing just three syllables,
two thousand years ago the crust
thinned over a lune of mantle,
and spewed a mouth of liquid rock skyward.
It pocked the earth with an oval hole
the native Ubehebe call a basket of stone,
gaping at the sky to be filled, and calling
to mind the womb of the pre-wed Maria,
who was rightly afraid of what by a fateful
waltz and a blush would be born in her.
Via the catacombs of the convent,
escaping capture and torture by Nazis,
she crossed over the Alps, steadily as a cloud.
Here at Ubehebe the clouds have stalled
above us, dark as they'd be in mid-storm,

and the pit we thought was barren blooms.
Rooted in cinders, the low shrubs grow
dark as char, and beyond them the blown rock
sums existence in striations: the dust we are
will lay its bone-white inch. Facing this,
why do we laugh like children? The two of us,
yodeling at that mouth, as though we were
totally unprepared for doom, as though our singing
could unleash a hellish quake, split the seams
of this place down to the core's original—
its rain of ash, its river of raw light—
alive, alive, alive, and on the move.

The Glacier on One-Upmanship

Gear gets sleeker
and then someone dares
a route no one's charted.

After, in the bar,
the victor sips her beer.
Her onlookers, who forsook
most comforts to feel
exceptional, fear they're normal.

At the table, each inches up
the decibel level
with tales of scaled peaks
and perilous traverses.

This makes her newness
something known,
something already owned.

On Trying to Save My Niece from Grieving

After my father
had recovered enough
to sit up in his bed,
my brother brought Clare in
to see him. He was losing
the tips of his fingers
on his right hand.
They were shriveled and black
above the knuckles—
the rough skin bent
at wild angles. As Clare
went to him, my father
(who could not lift
his arms) told her
he'd dipped his fingers
in blueberries,
and I watched Clare
measure the lie with a look
I have seen my whole life
on my brother's face.
And in how Clare
did not look away
from the wounds
on my father's hand,
but still reached out
to take hold of his wrist,
I saw my brother—
the way he can't help seeing
all our flaws,
the way he winces,
then for our weakness,
wills himself to love us again.

Skyline

Low clouds over the Shenandoahs,
a light rain on the stubble fields.
Under the white oak, noisy starlings

squabble in the dirt for seeds.
The month after your death, things move
above a winter ground. We look down

from a white-washed porch that's tilting
towards the center of the yard. There's
a red bird pushing through the box hedge.

There's a silence even birdsong doesn't break.
I am noting where the smokehouse needs new paint,
how the roof over the stable sags a little.

I am thinking there are few places in the States
this strange—a house that's been lived in
over two centuries, the bricks remarkably intact,

the grounds edged and groomed. We wanted to drive
out of the city, and drove here: Inn at Meander.
The ones who built it called it Elim. If we achieve

the unfamiliar land, the place your death is leading us,
even the common starlings will seem
to have more skill: black-gleaming oil and violet,

gathering in clans, pecking seeds from the dry earth
then all of them lifting into the air at once.

The Wasp on Kierkegaard

If you expect
the open air
  and find instead

your feet
fast in the dust
  so that you slip

at great speeds
down a hard sky,
  then love it.

Rebalance
on your three
  left feet. Extend

your right three
tenderly, tapping
  one black tip

at a time.
And the glass
  is good, as is

your belief
in its unseen
  edge, over which

you'll stumble—
unspanning
  on the force

of your own wings
(glass-free)
  and the grace

of the air
that was always there.

Excavating the Cyclops' Eyesocket

—Serifos Island, Cyclades, Greece

Inside the forehead,
bats hang upside-down
asleep in what they do not need to see.

I feel cold air
over my face as I stare
into the place light vanishes,

where I imagine some deep source
keeps clear and holy water
in a bed of stone. Meanwhile,

in a green and shallow pool
of the Aegean, a sleepless eye
inspects the sea.

Severed from the mind,
the eye neglects its duty,
and though it notes

the slope of sand,
the boat-swelled waves,
the pull and sway of seaweed,

and the silver, black, and blue-
striped, leaf-like fish that shimmer
into the eye's periphery, it lets them be.

I saw the eye from up above
while I was swimming. I watched it track
the shadow of my shape.

"Ancient Eye," I signed,
"How can you stand the sting,
this weighing sorrow?"

But the eye had survived many centuries,
and it didn't see the way I see.

The Sycamore on Forgiveness

You can't shake the thought that things
were better before the blast—
the slope gradual, the soil
concealing your knottiness.

Each rude train renews your ire—
a fire branching through your brain—
until you hate the fire more
than the trains, and you blame

yourself. How you wear your scars.
You're too hard, and you can't
will your anger away. You're
stuck on replay till the rant

becomes you (warped leaves, burled root).
You loot the soil. *You* strangle.
Then mercy schools you: green shoots
spring from the mess you mangled.

Old Dominion

Leontine Lowe, disguised as a hag, snuck behind
enemy lines at Bull Run, rode into the fields
like a peddler collecting brass buttons.

Through curls she grisled with dirt and oil,
she scanned the ground for bodies. Thaddeus Lowe,
the aeronaut, crashed his balloon on the wrong side

of the river. The stitched silk suffered a rip,
belled like a lady's hoop-slip, fell like a ghost-slow
spectacle above the smoke of musket fire.

Since there can't have been many trees
to conceal him, Thad hid under silks with a twisted ankle—
or, Thad had hidden the silks, disguised himself

as a dead man.

✳

A month after my father died,
my mom and I drove to Virginia. It was winter,
though eerily warm, a weather for the year

of fevers. We tried to book a hot air balloon,
not knowing we were thinking it would help us
escape into a lighter feeling, take positions

on the invisible air into which it seemed my father's spirit
disappeared, but the high winds kept us landbound.

✳

Because she knew the places she should look

but not exactly how Thad would be looking, Leontine
moved on the memory of him, and crossed into
the mortal fields where anything could happen, where

among the bodies that were lately marching
it was difficult to tell the dead from living.
And she found him on the ground, hid him from view,

then rode home across the marshes of Manassas.

*

The Occoquan splits through Bull Run,
disguising itself as a stream, in places it flows unseen,

erodes the ground, makes the hills unsafe for stepping.
Where it pools behind the flood-shoved boulder,
the river disguises itself as a mirror,

and the mirror disguises a soldier who disguises
just a man—of the body, and therefore doomed to die
(disguised as the sky).

*

Thad refused to fly untethered,

fastened his leads to a barge and followed the water.
From the air, he could see two rivers shining
like the seam of time, softening the ground with ditches,

threading through land that keeps the secret dead asleep.
Thad could see the borders of territory,
how the cavalry, riding drills, was shaped

by the shape of the land that was cut by rivers.
He could see soldiers hiding on either side of the river,
how they couldn't see each other, and didn't know

what it was that they were facing: death or victory.

*

The night before my father died, we sang him
Christmas hymns, we were singing him across

the terrible sea of pain, setting him afloat
on the loops of morphine while he unknit his spirit
out of muscle, blood, and bone. *Long lay the world,*

in sin and error pining. And up flew the soul,
into invisible. On a hill of names, from which you can see
the Capitol, above the steady roar of traffic

that follows a street shaped by the river,
under the shadow of the tombs of his ancestors,
my father's headstone marks the place we left

his ashes. And the granite, no one can move it,
though the wind and rain will scour it. I could tell you
I was certain of my father's passing, but it seemed

like he had joined the air, that giving up his body
spread him everywhere, and there was no place
I could go without him (though he's

impossible to see). Frail, consequential body,
matter that tethers our desire to be light,
what is it you'll do when the weird winds

turn amenable, and what we are leaves the disguise
by which we recognize each other? One by one,
we'll veer where love compels us.

The Wasp on the Golden Section

The best route is just above
the straightest line between two points.

There are arcs everywhere
in the air.

Perito Moreno Glacier

—El Calafate, Patagonia

One lost his hat to the wind—
it bobs on the surface of the jade-green lake
like a black gull. Clouds shift, the sound of lightning
echoes from the ice cliff, and a powder of ice
shakes loose, splashes. Two women clap and coo,
coaxing the glacier to perform, and it does feel alive—
heavy-tailed, befanged, and slow, cooling the wind
that crosses us as though it breathed. The pilot
speeds the boat to a melting berg, leans out
with gloves and pick-axe, hauling ice aboard.
He fills glass tumblers and when the wind picks up,
pours shots of whiskey on the rocks. On deck,
we raise our glasses to Perito, the Pleistocene's
most stubborn son, and when the whiskey's done,
while we look out at the glacier (its white forked tail
unfurling miles up Patagon peaks),
we chew a little ice between our teeth.

Notes

The title of "Embrace Them All" is a translation of Georges Brassens' "Embrasse-les tous."

"Northwest Passage": For some of the information in this poem, I rely on a Wikipedia article about Sir John Franklin, and his failed 1845 attempt to discover the Northwest Passage. In particular, lines 17-20 refer to the note the explorers left under a cairn on King William Island. The note was found in 1859 by Francis Leopold McLintock, who commanded the search party that Lady Jane Franklin personally commissioned (the British Admiralty organized the first search party, but when that search did not yield enough information, Lady Franklin enlisted "public commissions" to fund a ship and crew for a second search). The poem draws some imagery from a painting by Frederic Church, who added a broken mast to his painting *The Icebergs* as a tribute to Franklin and his crew. Special thanks to Anna Evans for her edits on this poem.

"Avalanche": In stanzas thirteen and fourteen, I quote two websites: <villatourism.com>, and <India.journeymart.com>. In stanzas 17-18, I quote a work that is cited in the *Oxford English Dictionary* entry for "avalanche." The *OED* sources the quote to Jrnl. Canad. Ling. Assoc. (1956) II. 28. In stanza 51, I quote the poem inscribed on the statue of Liliana Crociati de Szaszak in Recoleta Cemetery (written by her father). For definitions and etymologies in the poem, I quote the *Oxford English Dictionary*. Finally, I quote my father directly in this poem, as he identified the plant names for me.

"The Wasp on Renaissance Painters" is influenced by several Caravaggio paintings, especially "The Taking of Christ."

"The Soldier on Routine" was inspired by Elaine Scarry's *The Body in Pain*, and by a lecture given by Sr. Diana Ortiz, author of *The Blindfold's Eyes*.

"*Market Day Outside the Walls of Tangiers*" takes its title from the painting of the same title by Louis Comfort Tiffany.

"Old Dominion": This poem draws on the Wikipedia article about Thaddeus Lowe—an inventor who became famous not only because Lincoln appointed him "chief aeronaut" for balloon reconnaissance in the Civil War (a short-lived appointment, as it turns out), but also because of his later inventions, such as a new endothermic process to harness energy from steam and coal, an ice-making machine, and a scenic, "all-electric traction trolley" in Pasadena that ascended a mountain now named for him. In the poem, I am mainly interested in a single anecdote about Lowe's first reconnaissance flight during the battle of Bull Run. According to Mary Hoeling in *Thaddeus Lowe: America's One-Man Air Corps*, Lowe was forced to land behind Confederate lines. Though he was discovered by Union soldiers, he couldn't escape with them because he had twisted his ankle. Instead, the soldiers reported his position to Leontine Lowe: "Eventually his wife Leontine, disguised as an old hag, came to his rescue with a buckboard and canvas covers and was able to extract him and his equipment safely" (Wikipedia). In the poem, the details and descriptions I use to expand this anecdote are entirely fictional. While writing this poem, I read several other web articles including "War Watchers at Bull Run During the American Civil War" (historynet.com), and "Balloons in the American Civil War" (centennialofflight.gov). Also, I consulted the Thaddeus Lowe website frequently: http://www.thaddeuslowe.name/.

"The Wasp on the Golden Section": The Golden Section refers to a geometric system of proportion that can be used to measure or draw a shape and also to expand it symmetrically. The system relies on proportions in the ratio of 1: .61803, which is a ratio often found in nature (i.e. some of the ratios of parts to whole in plants and the human body). The poem is a tribute to the artist Dorothea Rockburne, who gave a lecture on the Golden Section and its influence on her work at the Vermont Studio Center in 2006.

"Pleasure Milker" is for Gary Braun, "String Theory: Pyramus and Thisbe" is for Davis Vardaman, "Before Edison Invented Lights" is for Maureen Horgan and Kara-Lee Ruotolo, "The Wasp on Archangels" is for Maria Hummel, "The Fire Balloons" is for Terry Quinn, and "Arriving at Ubehebe We Sing *The Sound of Music*" is for Kevin Tseng.

About the Author

KATY DIDDEN grew up in Washington, D.C. She earned a BA from Washington University in St. Louis, an MFA from the University of Maryland, and a PhD from the University of Missouri. Her poems have been published in journals such as *Ecotone*, *Smartish Pace*, *Bat City Review*, *The Kenyon Review*, and *Poetry*. She is currently a postdoctoral fellow at St. Louis University.

About the Series

The editors and directors of the Lena-Miles Wever Todd Poetry Series select 10-15 finalists from among those submitted each year. A judge of national renown then chooses one winner for publication. All selections are made blind to authorship in an open competition for which any North American poet is eligible. Lena-Miles Wever Todd Prize-winning books are distributed by Louisiana State University Press.

Previous Winners

Paradise, Indiana by Bruce Snider
(selected by Alice Friman)

What's This, Bombardier? by Ryan Flaherty
(selected by Alan Michael Parker)

Self-Portrait with Expletives by Kevin Clark
(selected by Martha Collins)

Pacific Shooter by Susan Parr
(selected by Susan Mitchell)

It was a terrible cloud at twilight by Alessandra Lynch
(selected by James Richardson)

Compulsions of Silkworms & Bees by Julianna Baggott
(selected by Linda Bierds)

Snow House by Brian Swann
(selected by John Koethe)

Motherhouse by Kathleen Jesme
(selected by Thylias Moss)

Lure by Nils Michals
(selected by Judy Jordan)

The Green Girls by John Blair
(selected by Cornelius Eady)

A Sacrificial Zinc by Matthew Cooperman
(selected by Susan Ludvigson)

The Light in Our Houses by Al Maginnes
(selected by Betty Adcock)

Strange Wood by Kevin Prufer
(selected by Andrea Hollander Budy)